ENGLISH FOOTBALL
AND MY (very small) PART IN IT

Stephen Hawkins

Published by New Generation Publishing in 2021

First Edition

ISBN
Paperback   978-1-80369-107-7
Ebook   978-1-80369-123-7

www.newgeneration-publishing.com

New Generation Publishing

THE STORY

This book is dedicated to my wonderful family and friends who have so generously suffered in silence whilst listening to my many speeches these past 45 or so years. So, I decided to stop ranting and start writing.

You know who you are xxxx

INTRODUCTION

My journey to this point is one of over 60 years of playing, following, studying and understanding the history of football and involves extraordinary amounts of joy, frustration, anger and tears watching England teams underperform (except for one glorious occasion) on the international stage.

A story that begins with England having created the modern game, then managing through a combination of indifference and intransigence to lose the head start it possessed and fall for long periods behind not only the great football nations but many others as well. The good news is that we are catching up again, and the task now is to stay there.

My own career was as a good amateur player who lacked confidence until playing in a senior team at 16. I improved in leaps and bounds and even had a trial with Crystal Palace at 17 who told me I was already too old. I was there with 13- and 14-year-olds who came with their mums and didn't even shower after! Disappointed as I was, the truth is I wasn't good enough but loved the game so much I happily carried on playing two to three times a week, summer five-a-side and anywhere there was a game.

I took my FA preliminary coaching badge at 23, which was unusual in those days (1977), as players at all levels tended to finish playing before beginning coaching. I passed first time, and as I prepared to obtain the FA full badge, I attended various weekend courses and coaching seminars at which I listened to so much nonsense I ended my coaching/management ambitions there and then (more later). Why I saw the game so differently to many who were already in the coaching field or taking their first steps made me question my understanding of the game and how it should be played. But although I was never to coach or manage, subsequent events have only reaffirmed and strengthened my philosophy.

After my playing career ended, a family came along and then a business opportunity which took me away from involvement in the game, but never ended my following, studying and being a fan of football, which continues to this day.

Such is my passion for football, I have on several occasions over the years told anyone who would listen that I would give up family, work and just about everything to manage England.

Obviously, no one listened, and that only intensified my passion to the point now where I need to tell the world how everything could have been different had the phone rung…

BEGINNINGS

I am going to keep this simple, as there is a history of peoples around the world kicking the stuffed heads and body parts of animals or human heads in some form of social activity or sport that could be described as predecessors of our wonderful game.

There exist numerous references to football-type games dating back to the ancients in China, Greece and Rome played with teams of varying numbers with and without what we might recognise as goals and scoring. A foot and ball appear in written and painted form together throughout this period to inform us of the birth of a sport. Thereafter through to the Middle Ages, games involving the carrying and kicking of a ball of various fabrications were being played in some form in Europe and other parts of the world.

But I am quite happy to begin my story about English football in our own green and pleasant land.

Versions of the games described above have existed in Britain dating back a thousand years and back then became a popular way to both socialise and settle differences between families and villages. Teams could be unequal, and outcomes sometimes settled by violence and damage to property rather than scoring.

Given these games had few rules and even fewer referees, it was not a game for the faint-hearted or the young. An intervention by VAR would not have been welcome!

However, the game in its various formats thrived and became among the common labourers of the day a national sport that rivalled and threatened our other national sport of the time… war! Men with any time on their hands were required to practise archery and other such wartime activities, as their lords or kings could at any time be fighting each other, invading or repelling invaders.

It's known that King Edward II (1284–1327) banned football to ensure archery was unchallenged as the main pastime of the male population. King Henry IV (1367–1413) imposed a tythe (tax) on places where the game was being played and banned the raising of money for it. The wording of documents at the time relating to the game quote the word "foteball". These kings were not alone as, over the subsequent 400–500 years, various monarchs followed suit in discouraging the sport.

CHINESE CHILDREN PLAYING 1130-1160

During this period, goals could comprise of posts in the ground or doorways of fixed points, buildings or forts, sometimes several miles apart.

The game did not evolve in any significant fashion during this period but became a little less violent and so began to be played more by the young. From the middle part of the 19th century, public schools in particular enthusiastically embraced the game in its raw form (including using hands), and there was a gradual emphasis placed on rules, team sizes and some form of pitch dimensions. The game began to more resemble what we know today as football.

As its popularity spread, so the modern game began to take shape, and as more schools introduced football to the curriculum, there were more participants. Competitions were introduced, and a game previously played in a somewhat chaotic manner was replaced by a more orderly, organised and tactical version.

Back with the adults, clubs were forming, created from works, hospitals, universities and gentlemen's clubs, etc., and matches were now being played by both adult and youth teams from different towns. The game was refining, and the earliest formations began to appear.

Regarding standardisation there was still far to go, as hands were still being used, caps worn (heading was still to come), and there were no uniforms or strips to distinguish teams from each other.

The first record of a referee came in 1842 at Eton school, and the first game with a timed length was played in 1846.

The first attempt to achieve standardisation occurred in 1848 in Cambridge, but no final agreement was reached on a set of rules, so different codes still existed in different parts of the country. The world's oldest club, Sheffield FC, was established in 1857, and even they created their own set of rules. Sheffield FC also lay claim to having invented the crossbar in the 1860s, which originally consisted of rope or string tied to the goalposts but was later standardised at 8 feet high and made of the same wood as the goalposts.

Now came early evidence of the theme of my story when, as the game in Scotland developed, it was being played more with the feet with an emphasis on passing, whereas in England, carrying in hand was still dominant. Eventually at a meeting in London on 26th October 1863, the Football Association (FA) was formed, and some rules of the game were established. Further meetings ensued where more rules were added, challenged and modified, with hacking being an interesting one!

Most importantly, use of the hands was eventually prohibited, resulting in the creation of Rugby as a separate sport. The size and weight of the ball was also standardised. There is some irony that as pitch sizes had yet to be standardised, matches were often held on open land and even cricket grounds!

The early formations were interesting and very attack-minded as in a friendly international between England and Scotland. England played with a 1-1-8 which was interchangeable to 1-2-7, whereas Scotland were more defensive with a 2-2-6 line-up!

There were still variances in the number of players in a team and other vagaries in respect of standardisation, as the rules the FA had created were not always followed, but progress was being made. The greatest progress, however, was in football's popularity. Clubs in some form had existed for over a century but were now being formed in their hundreds.

The working class rather than the public schools were now the driving force of this popularity. The advent of the railways made attending matches in other towns and cities easier, and games were now attracting crowds in the thousands. The game literally took to the streets with jumpers for goalposts, which was the original place of learning of the game for decades to come. We of a certain age can remember playing in a few of those.

By the 1880s, in order to win more games, clubs began to pay players to join their team. Selling tickets for games was a natural next step, and the game began its journey to becoming professional. The first professional club was Notts County, formed in 1862, and they were followed by clubs from the midlands and the northwest in general. In 1885, the professional game was legalised, and three years later in 1888, the Football League was formed, consisting of 12 clubs.

Demand to join was substantial, and in very quick time, new divisions were formed to accommodate new clubs. Meanwhile, crowds at matches were increasing to the extent that some attracted up to 30,000 spectators, and this then led to the building of stadiums: Bramall Lane, Sheffield, being one of the early examples.

Running parallel to all this was the creation of the first serious competition, the FA Cup in 1871, the first official international match between England and Scotland in 1872 and the first international competition among the home nations in 1883. British workers and travellers abroad were singing the praises of the new game as well as playing spontaneous games when running into fellow Brits. We had created a sporting monster, and the rest of the world was gradually won over by The Beautiful Game, especially in Europe and South America. Naturally, those emigrating to Australia and New Zealand took the game with them.

The game created by us Brits was becoming global, and football associations and leagues in various forms were appearing in Holland and Denmark in 1889, New Zealand in 1891, Argentina in 1893, Italy in 1898 and Germany and Uruguay in 1900, and other countries followed. So as the nascent game emerged, what followed in these countries was the birth of some of the greatest football clubs in history.

Now with the existence of clubs, stadiums, competitions and supporters, the game we all recognise and have grown up with was set to control our emotions like no sport before or since, producing immense joy and disappointment whilst at the same time determining the mood of individuals and entire nations for days, weeks and months at a time.

As the game spread around the world, it needed a body to oversee the standardisation of rules and the burgeoning international contests. Despite approaches from Holland and France around 1902, the FA remained indifferent to the development of the game abroad. At an official international match in Europe played between Belgium and France on 1st May 1904, the creation of an international federation was discussed. This resulted in the founding of FIFA on 21st May 1904 in Paris by seven nations – France, Denmark, Belgium, Holland, Spain, Sweden and Switzerland. Germany joined a few days later.

This in turn led to football being included in the Olympic Games of 1908 in London, where, although professional players participated (contrary to the Olympic principle), the game was well received by those attending and reporting. FIFA's first statutes empowered them with the sole right to arrange international matches. If it wasn't global before, it was now and has never looked back. Only the Olympic Games themselves can challenge the FIFA World Cup as the greatest sporting event on Earth.

It was quite extraordinary that after everything that had led to this point, England was not among the founder members of FIFA. The FA did quickly see sense and joined the following year but managed to fall out and leave in 1928 before the first World Cup over payments to amateurs. England finally re-joined after the Second World War in 1946 and have been members ever since.

FIFA now consists of six federations and 211 national associations.

However, as described above, we encounter further evidence of my theme, as at that time the FA did not see the need to join, given that we were already organised and had our own leagues and home internationals. FIFA had even adopted the rules as laid out by our FA, so we did not need anyone else to tell us how to run football. Having both organised and won the 1908 Olympic football tournament in London and then again winning the 1912 Olympic tournament in Sweden only added to our hubris.

I shall in later chapters further question and criticise the actions (or lack of) of the FA in terms of the development of the game both at international and grassroots level. But there is no doubt its creation was a worthy and necessary enterprise, with honourable motives, and as an administrative and governing body, it has successfully overseen the game in England.

The FA Cup of 1914–15 is an example of that. Despite men fighting on the front and criticism from some quarters, the FA, on advice from the War Office, went ahead anyway, as the boost in morale was considered worth it. Also to their credit was the acquisition of a piece of land in Wembley being used as part of the British Empire Exhibition in 1921. This led to the building of one of the most iconic sports stadiums in history, where the FA Cup final, World Cup final, Olympics and many other sporting events have since been staged.

After the First World War, the game went from strength to strength globally, and more nations and ever more clubs were participating in tournaments domestically and friendlies at international level. FIFA now also organised the competitions at the Olympics of 1924, which again attracted very large crowds.

The elephant in the room in all this was that the Olympics was for amateur players, and most of the best players were now professional. This, with the inexorable growth of the game during these years, along with the desire among nations to test their prowess against each other, only served to bring about what was inevitable… a World Cup.

CROWDS AT HIGHBURY STADIUM 1930'S

THE WORLD CUP... BUT IT'S NOT FOR US!

The creation of the World Cup was a no-brainer. Young men in their millions around the world were in love with a game that required technique, brains and speed. It allowed the imagination to create, both individually and collectively, beautiful patterns of play that sometimes took the breath away of those watching. Supporting your club or country became almost religious in its fervour, and the paraphernalia of rosettes, rattles, scarves and the like brought commercialism to the game in a big way.

As Eric Cantona said – *You can change your wife, your politics, your religion but can never, never change your favourite football club.*

The advent of radio now brought about an opportunity for supporters unable to travel and watch their team to still experience the emotional rollercoaster of a game, but with their ears instead!

The success of the Olympic tournament automatically led to conversations about a world tournament in some form, which was discussed at a 1928 congress in Amsterdam and later in Barcelona. As Uruguay was about to celebrate 100 years of independence and was emerging as a powerful force in football, having won the 1928 Olympic tournament, it was chosen to host the first World Cup in 1930.

Europe was in the grip of an economic crisis, leading some countries to consider the costs of travelling a long distance by boat (and perhaps returning quickly) and teams losing their best players for two months as too much to bear and so did not go. As was to be the case in future tournaments, the host country benefited from that advantage, and Uruguay duly won the 1930 World Cup and continued to be a world force for several decades.

OPENING CEREMONY 1930 WORLD CUP, MONTEVIDEO

Italy, now also a world force in the game, had lobbied hard to host in 1930 were piqued and decided not to travel, and the world was denied a potentially epic final between the strongest teams from two continents. However, Italy was rewarded with the second World Cup four years later, and it was obvious that their football development had been rapid as they won both the 1934 and 1938 tournaments! Again, the world was denied the final it wanted when Uruguay returned the favour and refused to participate in 1934.

Whilst some nations had various reasons for not participating in these early tournaments, England did not because we had left FIFA over the tenuous issue of amateurs receiving payments.

It appears most unfortunate that having created the modern game which the rest of the world had so enthusiastically embraced, England should now, at the triumphal fruition of its making, be absent!

The old adage of "You've got to be in it to win it" never rung so true. Due to their non-membership of FIFA and the Second World War, England were now not to participate in the very tournament its endeavours had produced for 20 years until 1950.

More's the pity that we did not enter the 1930 World Cup, as if the FA had been inclined, we had a readymade winning manager in Herbert Chapman. He had won the league title with both Huddersfield Town and Arsenal and, by competing, may have set the course of English football on a different path. Players like Ted Drake, Cliff Bastin and Eddie Hapgood of his great Arsenal team of the day among others were never able to show what they could do on the world stage.

All throughout this period, England continued to play friendlies (some not so much) against a variety of teams, achieving good results. Sometimes there was reason to field stronger teams than others, i.e., against Germany and Italy in the 1930s, but there was only one place to establish your standing in the world order, and our best young players during the 1930s were sadly denied this.

HERBERT CHAPMAN

Hardly any other sport can have such infinite potential to develop via tactics, formations and training as football, and this has been evident since those schoolboy days of the 1870s. To this end, a World Cup tournament was not only an intense competition but also an exhibition where nations showed the world their current style of play.

To participate was to experience up close where other nations were in terms of development. Players and managers could compare their technique, formations, tactics and speed and then recognise which areas of their game required improvement. All of this was unavailable to England.

The way teams prepared and whether their styles were defence or attack-based were all on show at the World Cup like products in a shop window. You could decide what styles or systems would or would not suit you or that you could adapt into your own style. The solutions were endless, BUT you had to be there.

As a further example of my theme, the FA demonstrated its reputation for administration via the organisation of the leagues and football at lower levels and had been, as a governing body, the world authority on the rules of the game for decades. But in terms of the international set-up, the England team was selected by a committee at the FA, and players were picked according to the whims and moods of the members of that selection committee. The development of tactics and formations at international level was not evolving, with real preparation not being a priority.

After the 1934 FA Cup Final, which he refereed, the FA appointed Stanley Rous to create a refereeing and coaching structure down through all levels. This improved things in terms of organisation and processing the better players through the system. The laws of the game were also rewritten and standardised. But what systems of play and techniques were being coached? Were they in line with current developments in world football or following the English methods of previous decades?

The end of the Second World War brought a renewed kinship among European nations with international games revived and thoughts returning to reinstating competitions. With the country feeling happier and experiencing a return to some sort of normality, club football was more popular than ever, and even with austerity, enormous crowds of around 41 million attended all the league games during the first season of 1946/47. England also re-joined FIFA.

From 1946, the FA looked to further incentivise the development process, with coaches and manuals being made available to clubs at all levels along with loans and publicity where appropriate. The FA council, previously intransigent, was persuaded to have a football "expert" on the board and to also appoint a Director of Coaching. Again, why was this never thought of before? This policy expansion now included the belated recognition leading up to the 1950 World Cup, that the England team also needed an England team manager in some form.

The man to fill both these positions (which the FA thought was good business) was Walter Winterbottom, the ex-Manchester United player. Winterbottom, who had also been a physical trainer with the Air Ministry, to his credit, introduced new methods of coaching, including a concentration on improving technique. His tactical knowledge was also very welcome, allowing for the understanding that there were alternative ways to achieve results. This could now be considered a watershed moment for English football to kick on and establish its arrival at the top of the game at the 1950 World Cup.

But wait a minute. Despite Winterbottom's minor earthquake effect on the development of our national game, it was still the non-experts on the FA committee who participated in picking the team.

Speechless!

WALTER WINTERBOTTOM

Our national team had always been strong. We were the best home nation team and had achieved good results for decades against many of Europe's strongest nations, but although we arrived in Brazil in 1950 with a strong team, we were novices at the World Cup and were now required to perform at the highest level when it really mattered.

Nations were then, as now, operating in four-year cycles. After each World Cup, there would be analysis by each country followed by a long-term plan involving the preparing of players and tactics to peak at the next World Cup. Due to the Second World war, this particular cycle was 12 years, but the principle of peaking at the right time remained.

Easier said than done. England, having achieved some good results leading up to the World Cup (beating Italy, one of the favourites, 4-0), arrived with high hopes, but after beating Chile in the Maracanã, we then lost 1-0 infamously to the USA and then Spain before coming home with our tails between our legs.

What was to be done?

WASTED YEARS – PART 1

Not much, it appears.

Having licked our wounds after the 1950 disappointment, there was a flurry of activity – meetings between the FA, club directors, coaches, managers and players. Topics discussed included coaching, training, preparation, development of young players, systems and tactics. Refereeing was also included, and there was a genuine effort made to put English football on the right path. The outcome was a better understanding between all those concerned, which helped improve things and laid foundations for the best young players to reach and play at the highest level their ability warranted.

However, there appeared to be no overwhelming desire to travel abroad, study the game's progress elsewhere and bring back ideas for development within our game. This had been an Achilles heel in England's outlook for decades and again contributed to more years in the international wilderness.

We see here again that England was talking to itself. If there was to still to be a big fellow up front who had the ball launched up to him for others to play off, then the best we could achieve was to get a better player up front; not really progress. The game in Europe was already developed to the point where our big fellow up front would be marked by another big fellow who had become a defender because he wasn't good enough to play up front in his country. They were producing footballers first and deciding their positions later depending on their ability and development.

The W-M formation which Herbert Chapman had introduced at Arsenal in the 1920s was still the basic formation, and players appeared to be produced to fit this system rather than having the freedom to develop their skills first and then create a system to suit.

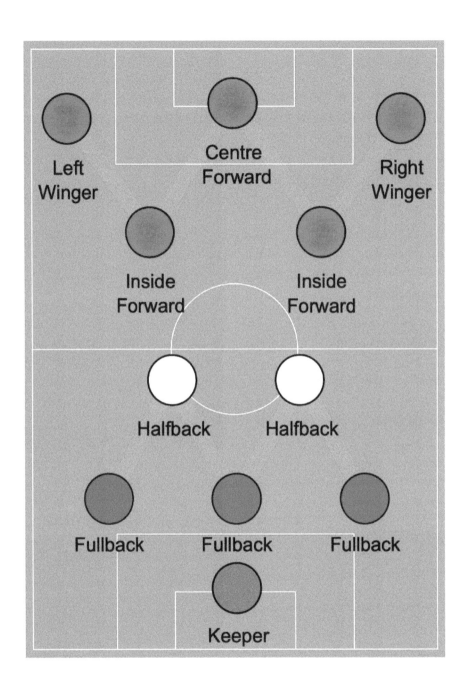

W-M FORMATION DIAGRAM

Meanwhile in Europe, my philosophy of how the game should be played was born. From the late 1940s to the mid-1950s, Hungary developed a style of football that suited the young players coming through (were you listening, England?) and became the precursor of the Total Football and possession football systems that followed. For me, it's a straight line:

HUNGARY (1950's) – AJAX/HOLLAND (1970's) – BARCELONA/SPAIN (2005-2015)

That is my football philosophy there.

Here, the Hungary manager Gusztáv Sebes (who had no real football qualifications) developed a club culture and spirit in the international squad, with regular training producing a real understanding and belief in the system they would play. He (not a committee!) also selected his squad from only a few clubs, as creating a winning team was more important than picking players on form. Given freedom to use his imagination, he could see the high technical ability of his players and encouraged them to interchange positions whilst keeping the formation. He trained the squad very hard, as the system required much movement, but his philosophy overwhelmingly placed technique and brains over strength and speed.

He also played without what was recognised as a centre forward, and these new innovations combined proved too much for all their opponents, giving defenders all sorts of headaches while forever pulling them out of position. Puskas, Hidegkuti, Kocsis and the others played one touch in triangles, creating overloads in which a Hungarian player was constantly free. Added to this was an emphasis on 11-a-side practice matches against senior league teams due to the limited time international squads were together.

GUSZTAV SEBES

Having gone back to the drawing board, England had regained some self-confidence by starting to win games and having some of its best players reaching their peak. While Hungary was now rated the best team in the world, England had risen from a low ranking to be rated third. A friendly was arranged at Wembley in 1953 and described by some in the press as "the game of the century." Hungary arrived unbeaten and were the Olympic champions. We also had reason to be confident with a team including Billy Wright, Stanley Matthews, Stan Mortensen and Alf Ramsey.

It was very one-sided with England struggling to have and keep possession and our players being manipulated by the brains and speed of the Hungarians, finally being reduced to a collection of confused individuals. The benefits of having the players together for long periods and training hard were clear to see, and the 6-3 score line flattered us. England had never lost at Wembley before, and the severity of this result ended the international careers of some that played that day.

Although there was some soul-searching by the FA after this severe setback, it did not produce the necessary shock to the system required to put us on the road to parity with the more advanced football nations.

A return match was arranged in Budapest the following year, to act as a warmup game for the World Cup of 1954. I was born on the day of the match in May but brought no luck to England, who suffered an ignominious 7-1 defeat which had repercussions for decades after.

FERENC PUSKAS AND BILLY WRIGHT, BUDAPEST 1954

Between 1950 and 1956, Hungary lost only one match, they won the Olympics, scored for fun, and their playing style was admired around the world. In the World Cup of 1954, they beat West Germany 8-3 in the group stage, who then somehow managed to survive for a rematch in the final. Questions will remain forever unanswered as to how Hungary allowed an early 2-0 lead to be overcome by a team who seemed out on their feet. But with help from the referee and a sudden burst of energy, which to this day has never been fully explained, West Germany recovered to win 3-2.

Politics and military matters put an end to this great Hungary team, which broke up as players sought to work at their trade away from the turmoil in safer and more rewarding nations.

No matter. While Hungary, in the same way as Holland 20 years later, could not claim to have the World Champions, there was no denying they had produced one of the greatest teams of all time.

Alongside this, Gusztáv Sebes could rightly be remembered as the father of Total Football.

It is not known if, after these two humiliations, the FA held an emergency meeting to set up a committee to put things right – to first travel to Hungary and study their development and training systems to understand how players and a team like this could be produced. Then to look at themselves and enact a root and branch overhaul, from the bottom up, of the entire coaching and youth development system with the single ambition of winning international tournaments.

We know, for instance, that after a disappointing performance in the 2000 European Championships, Germany did exactly that and produced the following World Cup results:

2002 – Final

2006 – Semi-final

2010 – Semi-final

2014 – Winners

Go figure.

HUNGARY TEAM 1954 WORLD CUP

The great thing is that football is forever evolving, and players and teams that excite are always arriving to grab our attention. At this time though, given its continuing expansion, the game in Europe was looking to consolidate its leagues and associations under its own ruling body. For once, excitement was created on the administration and governing side of the game.

To this end, on 15th June 1954, UEFA was formed in Basel, Switzerland, at a meeting attended by 25 nations as founding members and another six who were absent but included as founder members. This undoubtedly would have occurred earlier but for the intervention of two world wars pitting European nations against each other. But the timing was very good, as the game in Europe needed more tournaments for clubs to compete for and spectators to attend. As with the natural evolution of the World Cup in 1930, so it was with the European Cup in 1955.

There had been some competitions between clubs from different countries back in the late 19th century and sporadically since. But what accelerated the creation of the European Cup was the interest of two French journalists in cup tournaments in South America. There, there were cups for both the international and club sides on the continent, which contributed to the improvement in the quality of play at all levels. Needless to say, supporters who were still attending in great numbers welcomed it too.

You could forgive UEFA for thinking the worst as Real Madrid, with the incredible Puskas now lined up with the great Di Stéfano and Gento, won the first five European Cups as they liked. But clubs all over Europe were strengthening and rising to the challenge, and even before it manifested into the Champions League, it became the best club competition on Earth.

What did we in England make of all this? A mess, as usual. Given the repeated disasters experienced for decades through continued indifference and intransigence, you would have thought this was the great opportunity to test our best club sides against the best in Europe. And at the same time expand our understanding of how the game was developing elsewhere. We had not threatened at all to succeed in either the 1954 or 1958 World Cups, and had not entered the 1960 European Nations Cup, the first version of the European Championships. So, improvement needed to be found somewhere.

DUNCAN EDWARDS AT 16.

Our First Division at the time was being dominated by Wolverhampton Wanderers and Manchester United, yet there seemed very little enthusiasm or encouragement from the FA to enter the European Cup, as they still maintained an indifferent attitude to all things foreign.

Heads remained in the sand.

It was also unfortunate for England, when in 1958, tragedy struck Manchester United with the Munich air crash and the loss of eight of their exciting young team and two more with career-ending injuries. Among them was Duncan Edwards, a young superstar who was two-footed and happy playing in any position. He had great presence on the field for a young player, making him a potential England captain of the future.

As the 1960s dawned, my lovely dad Reg started taking me to games. Although an Arsenal supporter (he was born 500 yards from Highbury Stadium), he did not dress me in red and white or whisper Jack Kelsey in my ear while I slept but took me on alternate Saturdays to either Highbury or White Hart Lane. By 1962, I had fallen in love with the Tottenham double team, and that was that.

Meanwhile, the England team managed to reach the quarter-finals but were no match for Brazil in the 1962 World Cup tournament. It was also the year Walter Winterbottom resigned after 16 years as England manager. He had success as an organiser of the coaching structure but never really succeeded in improving and developing the style of the national team to make them competitive at the highest level. His inability to learn from the Hungary debacle, in particular, exposed his limitations. In his defence however, the FA didn't appear to care deeply enough about our status in world football and seemed content to continue enjoying the many benefits that being a member of the FA brought.

A wasted 12 years.

ALF RAMSEY

The FA certainly did not want to look inwards as a starting point for improving England's national team.

Among their self-serving rules was one that prohibited former or current players from sitting on any committees. And incredibly, the FA did not see how inhibiting this was to any chance of producing a coherent and progressive plan to improve our game.

But their comfortable existence was about to be shaken from the outside by someone they might have considered one of their own.

Alf Ramsey had been a very good fullback with good technique and tactical awareness. He was intelligent in that he timed his tackles well and always seemed to be in the right position, which earned him the nickname "The General". Having started at Southampton and gaining international recognition, he then moved to Tottenham Hotspur to compete for trophies. He was driven to win and even confusion over his age when signing did not stop the transfer. Tottenham were then managed by Arthur Rowe, who was among a few free thinkers outside the FA whose ideas centred around quick passes, one-twos and give-and-go football.

Does this ring a bell?

His ideas produced the great Tottenham Push and Run title-winning side of 1951, for which Ramsey played right back. He also played right back for England against Hungary in the first of those two heavy defeats and so, as a student of the game, would have learned much during this period.

Ramsey retired from playing in 1955 and went into management with Ipswich Town, then in the lower tiers of the English leagues. Under Ramsey there was continuous improvement, and after winning the Second Division in 1960/61, they were promoted to the First Division and duly won the title in their first season ever at that level. An extraordinary achievement.

Talk about the right man in the right place at the right time!

After Walter Winterbottom's resignation, Alf Ramsey's success made him an obvious choice, and after helping Ipswich through a few difficult months, he was appointed England manager in 1963.

As well as his tactical acumen, he was also smartly dressed and well-spoken like many of the "Blazers", as members of the FA committees later became known. His careers at Tottenham and Ipswich involved a lot of winning, and he did not need anyone to tell him how.

Ramsey immediately demanded and was given sole authority on picking the senior team as well as control of the under-23s, under-18s and all levels, and was not concerned about any noses he may have put out of joint.

As confident as he was managing, he was nervous with the press and not always on good terms with them. However, this did not affect his single-mindedness when it came to announcing that England would win the 1966 World Cup. Very early on, he named Bobby Moore, only 22 at the time, as his England captain. He developed the "wingless wonders" system where he did not play wingers but attacking midfielders who could also drop back and defend, giving the opposing team's fullbacks nothing to do while England attacked through the middle.

In 1963, the FA celebrated its centenary with an England v Rest of the World friendly at Wembley with Ramsey as the newly installed manager. Jimmy Greaves scored the winner in the last minute and could at that point be rightly considered among the best players in the world. His international scoring average – 44 goals in 57 games for England – remains unmatched, and he ranks among the greatest goal scorers ever.

I was 8 when I asked my mum to stitch a navy number 8 onto a white shirt, and I was Jimmy Greaves on every pitch and in every park and playground from that day on. He was and remains my hero to this day, and his recent passing was especially emotional and poignant.

However, Ramsey's tough decision to leave him out of the World Cup final team (there were tears from me) proved correct, demonstrating that for him, reputations counted for nothing against form, and you did not change a winning team for anyone.

ALF RAMSEY

JIMMY GREAVES BEATS THE REST OF THE WORLD, WEMBLEY 1963

England won the 1966 World Cup due to a combination of three reasons:

1/ England had the three best players in their positions to ever play for England before or since in the team at the same time:

Gordon Banks, Bobby Moore and Bobby Charlton

This world-class spine was extraordinary, and the records, reputations and standing in the game of the three players speak for themselves. A total of 287 caps.

2/ The best manager **England** have ever had, Alf Ramsey

See above.

Even when an inauspicious start made his prediction look shaky, he kept faith in his tactics. He also kept his nerve by playing Nobby Stiles despite pressure to drop him after a bad tackle against France and with the Jimmy Greaves decision.

3/ England were playing at home

England qualified automatically as host nation and could concentrate on being ready for the finals.

Before and since, host nations have strong records at either winning or travelling very far in the tournaments.

I remember after the final, my mates and I went to the local park and found some kids to replay the game against!

IMMORTAL 1966 WORLD CUP WINNING TEAM

It was not the most memorable of tournaments in footballing terms, in that Brazil and Pelé were kicked out, Italy knocked out by North Korea, and a ruthless version of Argentina turned up. France and Portugal with Eusebio played good football, and West Germany were their usual dogged selves. But nothing should detract from Alf Ramsey's achievement, given his bold prediction and the decades of struggle endured by England and its supporters since, when trying to repeat the feat.

We won the World Cup with a single-minded, driven, tactically astute and enormously respected manager who had no time for committees or the press, but always kept his promises! A fully deserved knighthood was bestowed on Ramsey in 1967, making him the first football manager to ever receive one.

The 1968 European Championship produced a third-place finish after a loss in quite a rough semi-final with Yugoslavia.

Two mistakes were to prove costly to Ramsey and England during the rest of his tenure as manager.

We went to the 1970 World Cup with possibly an even stronger team and were considered serious challengers to the all-star Brazilian team of Pelé and co. for the title. Even though it was played at altitude in Mexico and in very hot conditions, the squad was well-prepared.

BRAZIL 1970 WORLD CUP WINNERS

PELE HELD ALOFT IN 1970, MEXICO

Despite the missing jewellery distraction, Ramsey steered the team through to the quarter-finals via a tremendous match, which we lost 1-0 to favourites Brazil and in which Banks made "that save" and Moore made "that tackle", and we missed several chances. We continued to improve and outplayed West Germany at the beginning of the quarter-final match to establish a 2-0 lead. In trying to save Bobby Charlton's legs, Ramsey made the mistake of substituting him along with Martin Peters.

What Ramsey had perhaps forgotten was not how great Franz Beckenbauer was, but that he had spent the best part of the last decade playing deeper in order to mark Charlton. In the event, Beckenbauer went forward in his princely fashion and took over the game. The unfortunate absence of the great Banks in goal also contributed, and by the end of extra time, we had been eliminated.

The 1972 European Championship produced a déjà vu result with elimination at the quarter-final stage, again at the hands of West Germany.

In the 1974 World Cup qualifiers, England's group consisted of only three teams, including Wales and Poland. Although Poland was improving (and would go on to finish third in the tournament), it was still England's group to lose. The immortal team from 1966 was mostly broken up with only Ball, Peters and Moore still considered for international duty. Questions had been growing over Bobby Moore's play and in particular that his pace, which was never swift to begin with, had deteriorated.

In the away leg in Warsaw in 1973, Ramsey stuck with Moore for perhaps one game too many, and Moore was involved in the concession of both goals in the 2-0 loss. The return leg ended in a 1-1 draw with England needing a win to qualify, and despite the outstanding goalkeeping of their "clown" between the posts, the damage had already been done in Warsaw.

PELE AND BOBBY MOORE...RESPECT

Along with a gradual decline in the quality of play by England, these results hastened the departure of Ramsey, which occurred a few months later in May 1974. His disdain for any interference from committees during his tenure had possibly made some enemies who were happy to see him gone. Not a blazer after all!

His subsequent treatment was not that of a national hero.

We may never see his like again, and more is the shame.

A great man.

THE DUTCH YEARS

My extraordinary mum Tania was a Russian refugee who arrived penniless in London in 1951 after the Second World War and fell in love with and married an Englishman. She and the surviving members of her family group were transported from Russia by the Nazis on one of the last trains as they retreated, to carry on working for them in Berlin. After their liberation and some time in camps, most of the family decided to go to Brazil and my mum to London to be a nurse. My Auntie Muza had fallen in love with a Dutch refugee called Henk, and they went to live in Holland.

Everyone kept in touch, and eventually, mum and I went in the early 1960s to visit Auntie Muza and Uncle Henk in Amsterdam and had a great time. Then around 1968, we went back again, and by now I was football crazy, playing every break at school, for the school team and over the park literally in any spare time there was. We had won the World Cup and knew how football should be played... or so we thought!

While my mum and Muza gossiped away in Russian, sorting the world out, I went with Uncle Henk for some sightseeing and business meetings. A few of the days with Henk were boring, but then he surprised me with tickets to go and see the local football team play. We turned up at the old Ajax stadium with open terraces and a mad crowd.

What happened next laid the foundation of my football philosophy and my writing this. There in front of me were the young Cruyff, Krol, Suurbier, Haan, Keizer and the others and a form of football unknown to me. The rest of the world was also about to witness this remarkable style, which was to change the modern game.

Short passes, infinite movement and players appearing from nowhere in each other's positions. Comfortable in receiving the ball at any time with the technique to keep possession and move the opposition mercilessly where they did not want to be. There was also the similarity with Hungary in that they appeared to have no recognised centre forward or target man. It was so beautiful to watch it was almost football as art, which is how Johan Cruyff was later described.

I was only days old when Hungary so enraptured the world with their football, but I did not miss this and was an Ajax supporter from then on.

I followed them when I could on television as they reached the European Cup final of 1969, where they lost to Milan 4-1. I remember reading a newspaper report that said the Ajax system was possession without a final product and would not last long. I thought that once they started taking chances from the positions they were getting into, things would change dramatically, and they did.

Ajax were not the only team in Holland making a noise, and their great rivals Feyenoord beat them to the European Cup the following year, defeating the great Celtic side of the day 2-1. Ajax were not to be outdone and won the title for the first of three consecutive times from 1971, with Johan Neeskens now in the team. The Ajax system is the envy of many clubs in the world, where they take kids from 5 years old and teach them from the start to play the same way as the senior team so if they make it to senior level, they fit in seamlessly.

Along the way, they look for technique, intelligence and speed over physicality and encourage young players to play in and understand every position so they are comfortable anywhere on the pitch. They continually produce top-class players both for their own club but also others due to the economic pressure to sell today, caused by the smaller incomes received from television and sponsorship in Dutch football. Today it is harder than ever for Ajax to produce another all-conquering team, but my hope is they do, and we all get to experience their latest brand of Total Football.

JOHAN CRUYFF

43

Johan Cruyff was the star of Total Football and simply one of the greatest players ever. But Johan Neeskens is my favourite player ever. I believe he is the most complete player I have ever seen – first touch, pass, shot, tackle, dribble, heading, quick, two-footed, very brave and could play in any position. Ten Johan Neeskens and Gordon Banks was my dream team!

When I go to matches now, I make a point of watching the warmups despite most of the crowd remaining in the bars. I look for developments in the stretching, sprinting and one-touch formulas used nowadays to be game-ready.

Although a Spurs supporter, I could not miss Ajax playing Arsenal at Highbury in 1972. Warming goalkeepers up normally consisted of short, sharp shots at or close to the keeper to loosen and quicken his reflexes. Not for Cruyff, Haan and Keizer as they curled shots into the top corner and set each other up for volleys and half volleys, and the goalie was there to just return balls to them from the net. Talk about priorities! They still won the match 1-0 against a team who had won the double the previous year.

Back in Holland between 1972 and 1974, there began the golden years of Dutch football where the main stars from the two great clubs came together in the Dutch national team (see Hungary 1954). Jonny Rep was now added to the aforementioned Ajax group, and there came Rijsbergen, Jansen and van Hanegem from Feyenoord to form the core of the national team. At the same time, Rinus Michels had been appointed manager.

This became the finest team I have ever seen.

JOHAN NEESKENS

It says so much of the Total Football style that dominating possession was so dispiriting for opposing teams that when they finally had the ball, very little penetration was made as the Dutch simply pressed quickly and regained it. Such was their dominance of the enthralling 1974 World Cup tournament that leading up to the final against a very strong West Germany, the only goal conceded by Holland was an own goal by Krol against Bulgaria.

As a cat toying with a mouse rather than killing it, Holland, having scored a penalty with their first possession, did not finish off their opponents. You do that at your peril against West Germany (especially as the great Bayern Munich were now emulating Ajax with three European Cups in a row). Their refusal to lie down saw them gain a 2-1 lead, which despite the many chances created by the Dutch, they held on to in front of the home crowd.

Four years later in 1978 in Argentina, the fabric of the team was still intact with the addition of the van de Kerkhof twins from Eindhoven. The shock was the withdrawal of Cruyff on security grounds before the tournament started. But still this outstanding collection of players believed in their brand of football and again made the final. Here they again met the home team, brimming with wonderful players such as Passarella, Ardiles, Kempes and Luque. Argentina had earlier in the tournament participated in one of the finest football matches I have ever watched, against the young emerging French team containing Platini, Trésor, Bossis, Didier Six and Rocheteau, winning 2-1.

HOLLAND 1974, WORLD CUP TEAM

Despite political pressure, Argentina manager Menotti had in Ramseyesque fashion promised the country his team would triumph. Before kick-off, there was a hold-up as a cast on one of the van de Kerkhof hands was objected to by the Argentines, which held up play whilst being padded. Argentina took the lead through Kempes in a niggly match decorated by endless confetti. But for much of the rest of the game, they were forced back by the Dutch, who eventually deservedly equalised through Nanninga, and then could have won when Rensenbrink hit the post. But it was not to be as Argentina scored twice through Kempes and Bertoni in extra time to win the trophy.

Johan Cruyff had signed for Barcelona in 1973 and began the connection not only in terms of players and managers, between Ajax and Barcelona, but also in style of play, which continues to this day.

It should be said that through the decades, the Dutch have not won as many tournaments as they could have and have lacked mental strength at the most critical times. But their way of playing has had a profound effect on many coaches and managers that have followed, and their ideas and systems exist in some form in many countries around the world, including our own.

As Danny Blanchflower once said, this game is about the glory, and had Holland just won those two matches, there would be no discussion as to the greatest team of all time. But like Hungary, they had produced a team who will be remembered through the ages as one of the greatest. Brazil not only contributed the wonderful 1970 winners, but also the 1982 team that will be remembered as playing some of the most dazzling football ever seen but somehow managed to get knocked out in the quarter-finals.

In football, people remember not only who won, but who came second or even eighth...

Danny was right!!!

SCHOOLBOYS TO INTERNATIONALS – THE WRONG WAY

So, all through the early decades and eventual World Cups, while great football nations like Brazil, Italy, West Germany and Uruguay were winning two or more tournaments each and Hungary and Holland had produced two of the finest teams ever, how was the English game responding in terms of producing players and teams to challenge?

The answer was disappointingly little.

The head start English football had had from the 1880s onwards, when the game flourished at schoolboy level, was squandered as the adult game rushed on to professionalism and commercialism unaffected by foreign or domestic developments.

Football had grown and flourished, but in schools during the 1870s, teachers were organising games outside of school hours, as football was not yet fully sanctioned among schools' recreational activities. By the 1880s, football was on the curriculum and being played in schools throughout the country with competitions now established between schools, boroughs, counties and towns as its popularity continued to grow.

Then in 1904 came an important moment when the various loosely connected schoolboy associations looked to amalgamate into one central body. They wrote to the FA with a view to being brought into and under the direction of football's governing body.

They received back from the FA, the following reply:

I am in receipt of your letter (seeking permission to start a National Schools' FA) and enclosures. From the letter I gather that the proposed Competition is to be confined to Boys at School. This being so our consent is not necessary. We do not seek to control schoolboy football.

We do not seek to control schoolboy football…

From that point, the English Schools Football Association (ESFA) was formed and went its own way, and the opportunity for a top to bottom coaching and development system under a single body with unified aims and ambitions was missed. Both the FA and ESFA continued to succeed in their own fields thanks to competitions which attracted large support, but without enough attention to coaching and development of players.

This parting of the ways at such an important time for the game's development was a decisive moment which was to have negative consequences on the development of players for nearly a century.

What followed was the sacrifice of developing young technically and tactically proficient players for the long-term reward for short-term success in numerous competitions for 9- and 10-year-olds upwards. And this led inevitably to the type of players produced to represent England in the senior national side. Throughout this lost century, there came about a multitude of competitions for every age group across the country, always played on thousands of full-size pitches, which were the only places available to play on other than playgrounds.

Have you ever seen a 9- or 10-year-old on a full-size pitch? Sometimes a goalkeeper could barely clear the penalty area when taking a goal kick.

You could argue that some of the players in the England senior team were very often the direct result of the activities of enthusiastic teachers and parents. These enthusiastic teachers and parents were for decades via schools and local clubs, the managers of teams for 9- and 10-year-olds upwards.

Many had no real coaching qualifications or experience and most received no payment for their efforts. And efforts there were – collecting kids for the game, washing kits, taking practice, attending association meetings, sending in scores, phoning and chasing who was available and dealing with parents whose son could not get in the team!

What was their reward for all this effort? Winning, of course. A great sense of achievement would be felt if the local under-10 or under-11 Cup was held aloft at the end of the season. To achieve this, our manager would pick mostly the boys who could run the fastest, kick the ball the furthest, and physically go past or stop an opponent.

If a smaller boy showed technique and skills in the playground or training, he was not always considered when it came to that full-size pitch. How many potentially great players were lost to the game this way?

The boys who played in these teams would then get noticed by borough, district or county coaches and, when playing for those sides, were eventually noticed by professional club scouts and so on right up to international level.

But it was not the enthusiastic teachers and parents' fault that there were so many competitions, so many games and so many full-size pitches. This was the result of the authorities not looking outwards at how other nations were developing systems and players, as I have mentioned. Foreign nations had taken our game and refined it. It could already be seen in the major tournaments that the great difference was TECHNIQUE.

Here the other nations were developing footballers first, who could control and pass the ball long before they decided what position they might play in. What was important to them was how a young player aged 6–9 learned to play the game, concentrating on technical competence. Competitions and full-size pitches were not as important as ball skill development and would be introduced later.

A young player in England might turn up for practice and be told that the left back could not play on Saturday, so he was in the team. That young player might then move to another team and when asked what position he played, answer left back and for the rest of his playing career be a left back.

Almost every little boy in England is given a ball at some point. If they fall in love with the game (the first prerequisite), then all a 6- to 8-year-old needs are a ball and a wall. My own experience was with a tennis ball on the outside wall of my parents' flat. In this way, they can in their own time self-coach towards being technically competent, in an uncomplicated way.

From approx. 4 metres, one touch with the right foot against the wall as many times in succession until able to achieve approximately 25 consecutively. Repeat with the left foot then with alternate feet to create two-footedness. Then move closer to the wall in 1 metre increments and repeat, to improve reaction speed and technique until it all becomes instinctive and natural. This can be elevated to doing the above with half volleys etc. Then progress to kicking the ball from similar distances firmly against the wall and receiving the rebound with either foot, and moving off in any direction with just one touch.

It's not rocket science!

When a player has this absolute confidence in his or her first touch, he or she will go to any position on the pitch to receive the ball. That itself subconsciously creates a system of play where you and your teammates can move the ball from one end of the pitch to the other in any way you choose (Total Football?), and coaching becomes almost unnecessary. It is from here the game becomes beautiful as instinctive and unrehearsed patterns of play develop. Further patterns of play then occur that allow for the arrival of the right players into the right positions to affect the most damage.

Only good technique can achieve this.

Every football match is a story and each player's first touch a line in that story. If a player's first touch is good, then the next line is a pass, dribble, cross or shot as he or she chooses, and the story continues. If the first touch hits the shin and bounces 5 metres away, then the 21 other players, the 50,000 in the crowd and the millions watching on TV follow the ball, and so plot and storyline change.

There are countless examples of players through on goal and in other positions at a critical moment costing their teams dearly with a poor first touch, because:

FIRST TOUCH IS EVERYTHING

The result of all this was evident when watching the England under-16 side during the 1960s and 1970s when Schoolboy Internationals were televised. Here the English side achieved good results against the great nations, but it was noticeable that many of the English boys at under-16 level for the most part looked like grownups ready to play in the Football League, whereas the foreign teams consisted of several smaller, skinny types who were technically excellent but not yet physically developed. Sadly, most in those England teams were never heard of again at professional level, as they had peaked, having played all those games in competitions on full-size pitches and been fast tracked from 9 and 10 as described.

No one seemed to notice or act upon the fact that all those hundreds and hundreds of games played on full-size pitches in all those competitions between the ages of 9 and 16 had taken a toll on these children, because that is what they were. In effect, these boys had peaked technically and physically, and there was little or no improvement left.

This can only be the responsibility of the authorities, as the direction of English football was in their control, and that authority was never effectively used, as described here and in previous chapters. The long-term improvement of the game in England right through from the grassroots to the national team remained on the back burner.

WASTED YEARS – PART 2

As the nation who had created the modern game, we had also, after over a century, created millions of experts in the form of the fans and supporters whose weekly conversations and moods were determined by their local and the national team's performances. You could argue football exists inside the English DNA… It's in our blood!

Despite the regular discussions over who is the better team or player, we understand the game, know how it is played and know a good player when we see one.

There are "experts" sitting in working men's clubs, pubs and care homes who remember Dixie Dean along with Ted Drake, Alex James and Cliff Bastin up front for Arsenal (my uncle Stan, who's 94, for one) in the 1930s. They were followed by Nat Lofthouse, Tom Finney, Stanley Matthews, Billy Wright, Duncan Edwards right up to Banks, Moore, Charlton and beyond.

So, as we licked our wounds again after the disappointment of not qualifying for the 1974 World Cup, we asked, what was the plan?

The domestic game was thriving. Although, due to the enormous increase of car ownership, street football was in decline, football was still overwhelmingly the most played game in playgrounds and parks across the land. Crowds were still large, and the coming of televised games and *Match of the Day* had provided more ways to follow and form opinions about the game.

In 1963, Tottenham became the first English team to win a European competition (the Cup Winners' Cup) after a heart-breaking defeat by the great Benfica in the European Cup semi-final the previous year. West Ham followed two years later and Manchester City in 1970 in the same competition.

Manchester United crowned these achievements by becoming the first English club to win the European Cup with Best, Charlton and co. in 1968. All these teams played open attacking football. Celtic also played a free-flowing style and in 1967 had become the first British winners of a European competition, defeating Inter Milan 2-1 in the European Cup final, thus beginning the demise of the defensive Catenaccio system that brought success to Italian clubs during the 1950s and 1960s.

The home nations were persisting with the home internationals. Here they were still looking inwards at beating each other in fiercely contested end-of-season games when the opportunity to discover developments in the game abroad was available. They were later abandoned but had outlived their use by quite a few years.

Incredibly, up until 1974, England had only ever had two managers. From 1863 to 1950, the FA decided who should represent England at international level, and all these teams were picked on a who was playing well in our domestic league basis rather than who might be suitable for international football. As discussed, there was not much inquiring on their part beyond our shores as to what might be required to be successful at international level, where the game had clearly developed into a more technical rather than physical contest.

I had now obtained my preliminary FA coaching badge and prepared to go on to the full FA badge. I was raring to go and contribute to improving technique and tactics in the game at any level. But attending a preparatory course at Bisham Abbey was dispiriting. Ex-pros or those already in some coaching or managerial capacity were given an easy ride. Rather than asking those running the course how to improve as coaches, some attendees sat in question-and-answer sessions opining about the England team, which boots were the best and other irrelevant matters.

Watching a potential full badge coach begin a 15-minute session for heading for defenders with two touch, ball not above head height, really finished me off. But I had now witnessed first-hand where the English coaching system was after a hundred years of inadequate leadership, and it was not for me.

MY PRELIMINARY COACHING BADGE - VERY PROUD

There was so much evidence of the advance to a more technical game during the previous 25 years, first with Hungary, then followed by the success of Brazil and the Total Football of the Dutch. A chance for a new manager now existed to develop a squad of technically strong players from a young age through to the senior team with an emphasis on more possession to create more chances.

English domestic football had also over these decades seemed to forget the coaching principle of Space – Ball – Man and changed it to Space – Man – Ball, where players were rushing forward in front of the ball instead of coming on to it. These players of course got marked, causing an earlier breakdown of moves and teams unable to establish any patterns or rhythm of play.

The finest example of this is the goal voted the greatest ever, the fourth goal by Brazil in beating Italy 4-1 in the 1970 World Cup Final. After the magic of Rivellino and Jairzinho followed by Pelé's first touch, Pelé played an innocuous pass to his right, and we watching on telly wondered... to who? Out of nowhere and the TV picture came Carlos Alberto, and the rest is history. Space – Ball – Man. Watch on YouTube, and it all becomes clear.

Rugby union is another example where the laws do not allow forward passes, so players must hold their runs and come on to the ball. A fast-moving attacker has enormous advantage when arriving at speed onto a well-timed pass and hitting the space between static defenders. I used this in a session once, and the group saw my point and improved their positioning and timing of runs.

The intense nature of rugby union is also a reference point for commitment, discipline and most importantly, support both in and out of possession.

But it was not immediately to be, as the international side continued to struggle and failed to qualify for both the European Championships in 1976 and World Cup in 1978. As more managerial changes occurred, a lack of long-term planning was evident, but hopes were raised when a different type of player emerged…

Over the hill came a young player to excite all those experts who were waiting for someone who was technically excellent and would get them off their seats.

It was not only the experts, but we could all see Glen Hoddle coming. He had made his Tottenham debut as a 17-year-old sub in 1975. On his very first start in 1976, he scored a spectacular goal past then England goalkeeper Peter Shilton against Stoke City. One game, one goal, not an accident!

Hoddle flourished and after Tottenham were relegated, was instrumental in their immediate return to the First Division in 1977 and soon became a star back in the First Division. Alongside this, he graduated through the junior international ranks until making his full debut in 1979. He scored with a wonderful side foot volley from just outside the penalty area on his debut against Bulgaria. One game, one goal again… There's a pattern developing here!

He then went on over the next two to three years to be the fulcrum of Tottenham's progress to play in a League Cup final with Liverpool and reached the Cup Winners' Cup semi-final. They also finished fourth in the league, and along with scoring 19 goals in 41 games from midfield during the 1979/80 season, he won the Young Player of the Year award. At 22, this great talent should have had the international world at his feet. His instant ball control, passing ability and goalscoring with both feet were lighting up the First Division, and he was ready to do the same on the international stage.

Even allowing for young talent to be nurtured and not rushed, it was strange that he was only selected to start five times in the next 14 internationals played by England.

And in that fifth game against Spain, he scored his third goal for England with a volley from outside the box against Arconada, then considered one of the best keepers in the world. That was three goals in five games from midfield.

INSANE!!

But what happened over the next eight years encapsulated the story I am writing here. Hoddle was something different, and rather than embracing him, excuses were found not to play him – not quick enough or a great tackler, luxury player and not good at tracking back. The sort of things expected of midfielders since the 1880s. Colleagues at all levels expressed opinions that if he were European or South American, they would build a team around him. But that was never the England way before or much since. Other less productive and less talented players were selected in front of him to avoid having to make him the centre of everything.

Despite niggling injuries, he helped Tottenham win the 1984 UEFA Cup, on the way beating Feyenoord, where Johan Cruyff was now playing. Before the game, the great man was not sure what all the fuss was about with Hoddle but after the game asked to swap shirts… The heart bleeds!

In the meantime, Hoddle had not been in the first 11 in the 1982 World Cup, starting only one game in the first group stage and then watching from the subs bench as two goalless draws against West Germany and Spain led to elimination.

GLEN HODDLE

In the 1986 World Cup, Hoddle was given his chance and was influential in getting England through the group stage despite injury and a sending-off affecting his fellow midfielders Bryan Robson and Ray Wilkins. Their absence caused the line-up and system to change to Hoddle's benefit as he became the main man, and a must-win result of 3-0 against Poland saw England through the group stage and to a quarter-final game against Argentina. We know the rest with "the hand of God" goal followed by the "goal of the century", both scored by the immortal Diego Maradona, eliminating England.

Even as his Tottenham and England careers were waning, it was the great Arsène Wenger who bought him to Monaco, where he transformed their team and won several trophies. He was voted best foreign player in France to go with being voted into the PFA team of the year five times in the 1980s and into the team of the century in 2007. His goal at Watford remains one of the greatest two-touch goals in history.

His final total of only 53 caps remains a poor reward for his enormous ability.

Glen Hoddle is not the only example of this fear of the individual talent. Stanley Matthews, Peter Osgood, Alan Hudson, Tony Currie, Frank Worthington and, of course, Paul Gascoigne are among players whose individuality caused England managers headaches. Gascoigne was another player the experts could see coming. He had captained Newcastle's youth team to a cup victory in 1984/85 and later that year made his first team debut. By the 1987/88 season, he was playing regularly for an average Newcastle side, demonstrating that precocious talent which earned him the PFA Young Player of the Year award and selection to the PFA team of the year. His technical ability and ebullient play, along with a sneaky quickness, marked him out as an exceptional talent.

The 1988 European Championships required just five games to win, as only eight teams were in the finals. Split into two groups of four, the top two teams in each group went to the semi-finals and then the final. Although he had demonstrated in the junior England sides that he would soon be in the senior team, he was also quite unpredictable, not only with the ball but with his behaviour. With the World Cup only two years away, this would have been a great experience for his future development, to have been involved in a major tournament, even if he did not play.

PAUL GASCOIGNE

However, he was not chosen for the squad, and lesser players were selected. The tournament was another disappointment for England, losing all three group games and being eliminated. Meanwhile, the Dutch had produced another generation of great players including Frank Rijkaard, Ruud Gullit and Marco van Basten to win the competition.

When were we ever going to learn?

The 1990 World Cup confirmed Gascoigne as an outstanding international player, another one that you could build a team around. But that team could not be built, due more to Gascoigne himself than the indifference of managers, as he spent much of the next four years injured and unavailable. Without his mercurial ability to make something out of nothing and raise those around him, England were poor again, being eliminated from the 1992 European Championships at the group stage and not even qualifying for the 1994 World Cup.

The combination of the 1996 European Championships being played at home (without need for qualification) and a return to the centre of things by Gascoigne led to a very good performance by England, who were knocked out on penalties in the semi-final by eternal adversaries Germany. Gascoigne's two-touch goal against Scotland in that tournament was a worthy challenger to Hoddle's and cemented his reputation as one of the greatest England players of all time.

But sadly, between 1974 and 1998, England failed to qualify for the finals of three out of six World Cups, seemingly unable to change the direction they had been travelling in for nearly a century. And there remained an appearance of there being no plans to improve the top to bottom coaching system that produced mostly mediocre players and teams at international level.

These two great players had made it to the top, despite the system, not because of it!

Another 24 wasted years.

THE SMALLER NATIONS

Every time I've watched a game involving Holland, Croatia, Belgium, Denmark, Portugal or another of the smaller European or South American countries, I wonder if they are born technically proficient, such is their control and passing ability. It's possible that it's now in their genes but more likely they have learnt to play the game a different way over the decades.

In 1992, Denmark had been eliminated from the European Championships, and at the end of the season, their league games over, the players went their separate ways to the beaches and other holiday destinations around the world. Politics then intervened when Yugoslavia were disqualified due to events resulting from the breakup of that nation.

Denmark was reinstated, and urgent messages flashed around the world, asking players to stop drinking and overeating, and get home as soon as possible. The rapidly assembled squad then went on and won the tournament, on the way beating a powerful Holland team (who had won the previous event in 1988) on penalties in the semi-final, before beating a strong German (now unified) side 2-0 in the final. It helped that they had the great Brian Laudrup in the team, but it was an extraordinary feat by any standards.

Although they had played as a team and knew each other's games, they arrived without proper preparation. In the end, they had no choice but to play from memory and on instinct, depending on their technical ability and trust in each other.

When you have such a foundation of technical strength, anything is possible because it enables you to adapt or alter your system of play into almost any style. So it is with the smaller nations.

Between the 1930s and 1960s, these smaller nations were easier meat, as we had a more advanced game in terms of physicality and fitness, where we would outlast them in matches. In the ensuing years, they gradually improved their fitness and physical preparation for games, which they eventually paired with their technical prowess, and the results came. Added to the countries listed above are infamous losses to Norway in a 1981 World Cup qualifier and Iceland in the 2016 European Championships round of 16.

Croatia, in particular, has a population of just over four million, but scouts from all over Europe spend weeks and months travelling through the country looking for the next technically superb 13/14-year-old future superstar. And they just keep coming because the system produces them, and the national side punches above its weight accordingly.

There is also the great Ajax system discussed previously, in which its simple structure concentrates solely on the technical and tactical development of players from 5 and 6 through to their teenage years.

We, on the other hand, during this period, had largely ignored the need for technical development, which has been evident in most of the international tournaments in which we have participated. Now our advantage during the creation and development of the modern game has been nullified, the smaller nations play us without fear.

EXCUSES, EXCUSES – IT'S TECHNIQUE, STUPID!

Although we had the many experts already mentioned, who had attended matches over the decades and witnessed the coming and going of the great English players, we now had television.

Since the mid-1950s, families had slowly begun to drift from radio and invest in this new medium for entertainment. Along with the news and shows came live and recorded sport, which in terms of football created a whole new type of expert, the armchair expert.

Whilst we could now watch and form opinions from the comfort of an armchair, those providing the sport felt we needed more information and opinion to digest and provided this through the introduction of the pundit. The pundits have since the early days consisted, in the main, of a presenter accompanied by a combination of personalities from the game in the form of ex or current players and ex or current managers. These experts help where possible with opinions and insight, formed by their experiences in the game, and contribute to the daily conversations across our football-mad country.

The press has also provided ever more coverage of the game and employed pundits with daily and weekly columns not only reporting on matches but delivering articles and opinions of all kinds to back up their views of the game.

Add to all this, Twitter, Facebook, numerous blogs and various other social media platforms, and you have an enormous, bewildering range of information to assist you in forming your opinions on every aspect of the game.

However, before the dominating entrance of the internet over a decade ago, a combination of some people in football, some pundits and some of the press arrived at two very strong opinions as to why the England team had underachieved over such a long period since 1966. These gained traction and appeared to be generally accepted as contributing to our standing in world football. I could not understand this.

1/ Too many foreign players

The reasoning was that foreign players were taking the places of English players in teams, denying more of them a chance to play and develop into potential internationals.

There is evidence of the odd foreign national playing in the early 1900s and in the following years of further individuals appearing for clubs, but these can be counted on the fingers of two hands. But in 1930, the Ministry of Labour issued an edict to the effect that clubs could not employ foreign nationals due to the high levels of unemployment in the country at that time. This did not meet with any objection from the FA, and so football was almost totally played by home-grown talent.

Thinking back to 1950 and our first World Cup, followed by humiliation at the hands of Hungary three years later, there is not much evidence of English clubs during those years importing, in any meaningful way, players from Europe and South America to play in the English league. So, the answer to our struggles at international level at that time must lay elsewhere, but where?

Moving forward to the late 1950s and 1960s, there is still no record of this happening in any great numbers. Bert Trautmann, the great German goalkeeper, managed to win Footballer of the Year in 1956, but otherwise there was still no large influx of foreign talent.

But here you could argue that for 60 years until our triumph in 1966, players such as Alex James, Jon Charles, Dave Mackay, Cliff Jones, Dennis Law and George Best among many others were "foreigners", keeping English players from succeeding in the professional game. Should we have barred them from playing in England and missed the joy and pleasure they brought to our game, for the sake of maybe improving our international prospects? The answer is obvious.

From the 1970s onwards, our membership of the EU obligated us to trade on their terms in allowing all member state citizens to ply their trade anywhere within the community. The commercial aspect of the game was now ever more important in that qualifying for European competitions was very rewarding with television rights etc. There was now also opportunity for importing *overseas players with established international reputation, who have a distinctive contribution to make to the nation's gam*e, according to the authorities. After Tottenham's signing of Osvaldo Ardiles and Ricardo Villa from Argentina, the trickle did not turn into a flood immediately but steadily increased, especially after the later Bosman ruling.

But before the introduction of Tottenham's two signings in 1978 and the beginning of the influx of foreign players to follow, it must be remembered that England had failed to qualify for both the 1974 and 1978 World Cups. So, again the answer to our struggles at international level must lay elsewhere, but where?

Since then, it is indisputable that foreign players have embellished our league, transforming it into one of the world's finest. Children playing the game at an early stage try to emulate their techniques and tricks to improve their ability and ball skills generally. In turn this has helped, in a subliminal way, young English players coming into the Premier League to be technically more proficient than their predecessors. This is wonderful.

2/ Too many games

I'm not sure if this excuse preceded, succeeded or ran parallel to the one above but believe it has been provided in equal measure as a reason for our poor performances at international tournaments.

Its reasoning is that the English season is longer than most with no winter break. Extra competitions and international matches add to the toll on limbs and energy levels of players.

As a young player in my 20s, I was a football addict and, like most of that age, considered myself indestructible. Three games a week in three different leagues (occasionally on consecutive days) plus training was my fix. Doing the thing I loved most in the world was heaven, and I could not wait for the next game. The more games you play though, the more chance there is of injury, and I had my fair share of those. But professional players are no different, still young men doing the thing they love most, and their mantra has always been the same as ours in preferring playing to training.

At professional level, the game is faster, and collisions can have more serious consequences on the body. The English game has always been known to be among the most physical going back to the earliest days. Then squads were smaller, and players had no real opportunity to be rested, so carried on playing through fatigue and injury.

Throughout the years, due to the arrival of commercialism and sponsorship along with more competitions at club and national level, squads have been enlarged to accommodate the extra matches, providing an opportunity to rest players at various times. Improvement in equipment, training regimes, facilities and treatments have contributed to conditioning players better and producing shorter recovery times from injuries.

Over the last 30 years, with the coming of the Champions League and including internationals, players at the top clubs throughout Europe have become used to and prepared to play 50–60 times a season, occasionally more. For South American players, many also employed in the Spanish, German and Italian leagues, this includes return flights in the middle of a season to their home countries in different time zones, adding to fatigue. This is now accepted as the norm, with dieting and conditioning playing an important role in maintaining fitness. To this extent, current coaching qualifications require an understanding of dietary and injury aspects as well as tactics and technique, and this is all to the good.

For me there is one overriding reason for the generally poor performances at international level by England teams through the decades, and I have mentioned it several times – TECHNIQUE.

If you spend 90 minutes running flat out chasing the ball, tackling, recovering it, losing it, chasing again, etc., you are going to suffer. This was the foundation of our game for a century.

If for 90 minutes you can keep the ball and move it from one end of the pitch to the other, and then regain possession quickly, your opponents are going to suffer, i.e., England.

To keep possession requires two things; the ability to control the ball and the ability to pass the ball. These demand that a player has good technique, and the critical point is…

FIRST TOUCH IS EVERYTHING.

We cannot hide from the fact that from the earliest days in the 1880s, we in England have done things our own way and ignored for decades, to our own cost, the direction the rest of the world has travelled. There, they do not look at the size or power of the player, only their technique, intelligence and speed.

THE HOLY TRINITY OF GREAT SMALL PLAYERS

The great Iniesta/ Xavi partnership is a good example of this. Their size made no difference because no matter what your tactics of dropping off, pressing or man marking are, their first touch, technique and intelligence ensured they and their team dominated possession. Their quickness over 5 yards (the most important in football) enabled them to evade the most determined of markers.

It also helped that they had someone called Lionel Messi and a few others, but I reason they would have improved any team they played for.

Michel Platini, Alain Giresse and Jean Tigana of the great French team of the 1980s are another example of players of no great height or physique, who dominated possession through technique, intelligence and speed, and provided their colleagues with so many scoring opportunities. If only they had had a proven goal scorer to take the chances they created, a World Cup might have been theirs.

Players with great first touch have appeared throughout the decades in both England and on the continent. The likes of Greaves, Best, Hoddle, Brady, Dalglish, Cantona, Zola, Bergkamp, van Persie and others have been able to create something out of nothing in English football with one touch. They all played with their heads up, deciding what they were going to do with the ball as it came rather than worrying about controlling it. In the same way, basketball players in the USA never look down at the bouncing ball because their control is absolute, and they are looking around the court and at their next move. Such is the benefit of good technique. This ability to play with their heads up often leads to players being described as having great vision, but for me it's just great technique that allows them time to see and make a decisive pass. We can also reference basketball, firstly for being the origin of the press, now a key tactic in modern football, and secondly for the screen, used for blocking defenders from staying with attackers at set pieces.

But it is the technical ability of all 11 players on the pitch combined that enables teams to enjoy ball retention and dominate possession. If there is one or more weak links technically, then a team will lose possession more often and be forced to chase the ball, causing physical and mental fatigue. Dominating possession allows a team to create their own rhythm, speeding up or slowing down when necessary and playing the game at the pace it chooses.

A good way for any coach arriving at a club in the lower levels to quickly assess the abilities of his or her players is a game of two touch. Thirty minutes of two touch will demonstrate the technical, tactical and work ethic levels of any squad and provide the coach with a starting point for their work. This should not be necessary at professional or international level.

The game is so much easier to play with the ball than without it.

Penalties are sometimes blasted as hard as possible, but most are taken by passing the ball into the net. It's simply a firm 12-yard pass or shot into one corner of the goal, a technique that we all have. But when the pressure is on, everyone gets nervous, and here you must trust your technique to the limit. The side netting is a perfect target which even a diving keeper may not reach. But in the past, we have seen our international players suffer more than others because their trust was not as complete as their opponents and their technique failed them at the vital moment.

It is the average technical ability of English players that has needed improving for decades so that our international team could be competitive at tournament level. This goes back to how they are taught and coached in the game during those early years and subsequently, as I have outlined in previous chapters.

This is something that is now happening, and as we become technically equal to other nations and add the English character attributes of big hearts and endeavour, then the time to challenge consistently for success at international level will have arrived.

THE FA, ENGLAND MANAGERS AND OPPORTUNITIES MISSED

It must be acknowledged that in all its 29-year history, no English manager has ever won the Premiere League.

It could be said that through the decades, English players and managers, with only a few exceptions, have travelled the same path in international football in not possessing the technical, tactical and analytical quality required to succeed at that level. Over the years, this has resulted in the importation of many top foreign players and managers into the Premier League rather than the other way round.

This cannot continue and is a direction of travel we hope our continuing improvement in players' technique and development of young managers will slow down or even reverse.

I have always believed, rightly or wrongly, that the England manager position is very straightforward compared to a club manager. You do have extraordinary pressure, as the mood of the nation rests on your shoulders, depending on the team's performances. But there is every reason for an individual with a combination of experience, confidence, determination and knowledge, with good man management skills, to succeed. Think of Ramsey.

You have an enormous pool of talent to choose from. You do not have to negotiate contracts. You do not have to worry about the sudden transfer of star players. You do not have any pre-season or fitness regimes to implement, and players normally arrive ready to play. You have at your disposal the best facilities and the choice of watching who you want when you want at club level, particularly young players developing fast. There is only one competition every two years to plan, prepare and compete for.

Success depends on your judgement of which players are suitable for international football and your further judgement of which system of play most suits their capabilities. You must then implement that system, with the players buying in and understanding it completely. Finally, you must be able to prepare, organise and motivate your squad to achieve the best possible results.

But best of all, it allows you to concentrate on doing the thing you love most... coaching.

It's a dream job.

You would have thought that from its creation in 1863 through to employing its first international team manager Walter Winterbottom in 1946, the FA would have had enough time to establish such a criterion to be met by any candidates. Playing record, experience and success rate in management, style of play, age and character, etc. could all be considered when selecting someone to manage the national team of the country that created the modern game.

This does not seem to have been the case. The FA had only reluctantly decided to have an expert on the ruling council, and Walter Winterbottom, who had no previous football management experience, was selected to fill two positions – Director of Coaching and England team manager.

Here we see that winning an international tournament was still not the highest objective of the FA. To compound this, without an ex-player or manager on the council, they still insisted on selecting the squad and team, with Winterbottom only allowed to argue the case for players along with two committee members.

His record was a good one after the 1950 World Cup early exit. But he perhaps had greater success in his second job as he set up the first truly top to bottom coaching system in England which improved techniques. This was achieved via manuals and improved coaching at all levels, which created a path for good young players to travel from schoolboy level to the professional game and progress through the various international teams.

But after the early exit from the 1950 World Cup, an opportunity existed to have Walter Winterbottom concentrate on his excellent administration of the nation's coaching system and appoint someone with the sole responsibility of managing the national side.

Arthur Rowe had been a decent player but more importantly had had success in management, first with Chelmsford City and then Tottenham Hotspur. Extraordinarily, after his playing career ended, he obtained a coaching position in Hungary, which was interrupted by the Second World War. There he was, in the birthplace of the Magyars of Hungary whose style took them to the pinnacle of world football.

Their style obviously left an impression, as he went on to manage Tottenham to win the Second Division and First Division titles in consecutive seasons up until 1951, with that wonderful Push and Run team playing a similar style to the Hungarians…

It is not known if the FA ever approached Rowe or whether Tottenham would have released him. But how interesting if he as England manager had played against Hungary with a team playing the Magyars at their own game! And how different the road English football might have travelled from then on. An opportunity possibly missed.

Rowe had to retire from management in 1955 for health reasons and although returning in a lesser capacity in 1958 with Crystal Palace, he suffered more with his health for the rest of his career.

The next managerial decision the FA made was their best ever. It was in an era of great English managers, including Bill Nicholson and Stan Cullis, so the decision to appoint Alf Ramsey turned out to be a great one. Alf Ramsey was successful as a player with Tottenham and as a manager with Ipswich and so it proved with England, and his merits are discussed elsewhere.

Along with winning the World Cup, perhaps his greatest achievement with England was to finally separate the selection of squads and players from the FA and begin the era of all playing responsibilities being in the hands of the manager, including travel plans etc. He had repeated the achievements of Arthur Rowe by winning the Second and First Division titles in consecutive seasons, something that was for some reason ignored by the FA when searching for a manager some years later.

ARTHUR ROWE

TOTTENHAM HOTSPUR 1951 CHAMPIONS

And Ramsey, like Rowe… was a winner.

On Ramsey's departure, a caretaker manager, the very experienced Joe Mercer, was appointed, who only lost one game in seven but was not asked to stay on a permanent basis, as the FA wanted Don Revie. Revie was a winner, and on his appointment, big things were expected but never really materialised, as his football was pragmatic (including dossiers on the opposition), with never a settled side and an embarrassing defeat to the great Holland side of the time. He eventually jumped ship for a highly paid job with the United Arab Emirates, which caused legal issues with the FA and dented his reputation.

On Revie's resignation in 1977, there came an opportunity to appoint one of the greatest club managers of all time, Brian Clough. It wasn't as if he needed to be asked, he actually applied!

As a player, he had the world at his feet, developing into a very skilful forward with one of the greatest scoring averages ever, scoring 204 goals in 222 games for Middlesbrough and 63 in 74 games for Sunderland. Having played twice for England, his career was sadly curtailed by serious injury.

His managerial career was nothing less than outstanding, despite two hiccups at Leeds and Brighton. He started at Hartlepool, where he drove the team bus and went round local pubs and clubs raising money to keep the club solvent and in the league. They survived and eventually achieved promotion thanks to his efforts.

Moving to Derby, he built a team, including players who would both follow and run through brick walls for him. His judgement of players was generally proved right, and he added signings which led to Derby winning the First Division title for the first time in their history and contesting a European Cup semi-final against Juventus. He wasn't afraid to speak his mind and fall out with anybody, and that eventually led to his leaving Derby.

What stands out is that no matter how often he was knocked down, his immense belief in his own ability never wavered, and to prove the point, he went and overachieved again at Nottingham Forest. Here he had a familiar core of players but added the likes of Peter Shilton and Trevor Francis to create the greatest period in their history, winning multiple trophies. Clough repeated the feat of promotion from the Second Division and winning the First Division in consecutive seasons achieved by both Arthur Rowe and Alf Ramsey. He further managed to beat the great Liverpool side of that time in the league, the League Cup and also knocked them out of the European Cup after they had won it in the previous two seasons.

These occurred after he had applied and been turned down for the England manager position. It goes without saying, he would have shaken up the staid world the FA occupied and wearing a blazer was not for him. His football was good to watch too, based on a passing game, keeping the ball on the ground and dominating possession, famously saying, "If God had wanted us to play football in the clouds, he would have put grass up there."

He ranks alongside Matt Busby, Alex Ferguson, Bill Shankly and Bill Nicholson as one of the greatest motivators in English football, and unequivocally, he was the best man for the job at the time. But the FA inexplicably overlooked him to the detriment of English football.

As with outstanding individual players, so with a mercurial manager, there existed a fear of anything that might rock the boat and disrupt the status quo the FA had enjoyed for decades.

A wonderful opportunity missed.

In an era of outstanding English managers, someone who had achieved even greater success than Brian Clough was Bob Paisley of Liverpool. This very modest man had quietly taken over from the great Bill Shankly, who had brought Liverpool from the Second Division to the top of English football.

BRIAN CLOUGH

Having served in the Second World War and afterwards played for Liverpool, he started at the bottom of the coaching staff. After attaining physiotherapy qualifications, his understanding of injuries and recovery methods contributed to the fitness and conditioning of the first team. He was also an advocate for training with a ball as against just running to achieve fitness. This meeting of minds eventually led him to become assistant to Bill Shankly and an important member of the famous boot room meetings, which discussed the players, team and tactics for coming matches.

In 1974, in the interests of continuity, he was asked to succeed Shankly and reluctantly agreed. Even though he had big shoes to fill, between 1974 and 1983, he led Liverpool to no less than 20 major trophies and took the club to the summit of European football, on the way becoming the first ever manager to win three European cups. The clashes with Nottingham Forest and Brian Clough during this period provided many memorable matches for us fans to enjoy.

With this extraordinary record, he was more than qualified for international football. It's not known if he or Liverpool were ever approached by the FA for the England manager position or whether he would have accepted or been released by Liverpool.

He was one of the greatest ever English managers.

Good managers like Ron Greenwood (of the excellent West Ham team of the 1960s) and big-hearted Bobby Robson (manager of the splendid Ipswich team), who took England to the 1990 World Cup semi-final, could not take England to the next level in terms of international player development. The blame for this could not be put on them, as there simply was no conveyor belt of high-quality technical players coming through the system to enable England to challenge the likes of Argentina, Brazil, Germany and Italy on a regular basis.

The FA did not have a large field of candidates to replace Bobby Robson and settled on appointing Graham Taylor, whose club record was not outstanding and whose style of football was based on the long ball. Although possessing a love of the game and a big heart, his tenure was unsuccessful, with an exit at the group stage of the 1992 European Championships and failure to qualify for the 1994 World Cup. If we were hoping for a manager who understood what was required at international level, there now followed two very strong candidates...

Football is a game where the techniques of controlling the ball (first touch) and passing the ball are fundamental. The higher the level the game is played at, the more important these techniques become. So, you arrive at a judgement that you need a particular type of player at international level and pick those suitable as against who might be playing well at club level. Terry Venables and Glen Hoddle appeared to recognise this and developed their teams and styles in this way.

Looking back, there are many examples of good managers recognising a player's ability in the lower levels or non-league football and realising it would blossom when that player played at a higher level in a stronger team that would enhance their qualities. Kevin Keegan, Alan Devonshire, Gary Birtles, Graham Roberts and Cyril Regis are just a few examples of this, and they all went on to be internationals.

It is also the case at international level, where ball retention is so important. Venables and Hoddle both understood this and managed the England team accordingly. Venables, who had played for England at every level and managed the great Barcelona, coached England to the semi-final of the 1996 European Championships, on the way destroying a strong Holland side 4-1 in one of England's finest performances ever. Chances missed were costly as England went out on penalties against Germany in the semi-final. A foundation had been laid but sadly was prematurely abandoned for off-field reasons.

Hoddle had been a fantastic player (see earlier) and towards the end of his playing career was bought by Arsène Wenger to play in Monaco. To have been at the start of Wenger's wonderful managerial career must have been enormously informative to Hoddle. He arrived at the England manager position via creating attractive playing teams at Swindon and Chelsea, where the emphasis was on possession and controlling games.

There was promise in the development of the England team and style, which led them to playing tremendously well in the round of 16 in the 1998 World Cup against a good Argentina side. Unfortunately, despite being down to 10 men and surviving extra time, they were knocked out of a tournament for the second time in two years on penalties. Hoddle's win ratio of 60% as England manager was bettered only by Alf Ramsey and Fabio Capello.

But as with Venables, so with Hoddle, there was much to build on, and again for the second time in just a few years, a potentially promising future for the England national side was brought to an abrupt end due to off-field issues.

More opportunities missed.

However, the FA did finally begin to see the light in respect of the need to develop and prepare the best young players for international football via a specific programme for that purpose. To this end, there followed a pivotal moment in the English game, which could be said to have been the first step on the road to where we are today, and it was brought about by Howard Wilkinson.

Wilkinson had not been an outstanding player but achieved success as a manager, first gaining promotion from the Second Division with Sheffield Wednesday and then with Leeds United. In three seasons, he took Leeds from the Second Division to being First Division champions. His installation of discipline, good coaching and shrewd activity in the transfer market brought the club back to the top of English football. However, he was subsequently unable to sustain them at the top but remains the last English manager to win the First Division.

He was a student of the game and took an interest in developments abroad, particularly the development of elite young players. Here he found that in many countries, there existed some form of academy or centre of excellence dedicated to the production of players to be successful at international level.

After leaving Leeds in 1996, he was appointed a few months later in January 1997 by the FA as Technical Director. After listening to his ideas, the FA bought a plot of land for the explicit purpose of creating a Centre of Excellence, which we know today as St George's Park. They also asked him twice to be caretaker manager of the England side.

During this period, he concentrated on the Centre of Excellence, which it was hoped would emulate the French National Football Centre at Clairefontaine, which had produced the players that won the 1998 World Cup and European Championships in 2000. It took quite a few years to come to fruition (due to the building of the new Wembley) but was finally opened in 2012. Around this time, Gareth Southgate had been appointed head of elite development (more later) at St George's Park.

Added to the world-class facilities were the introduction of aspects of the game previously not given enough attention, including sports sciences, psychology and analytics. England now finally had a place to take a long-term view on the development and preparation of young players to succeed at international level. Long term was the key part of the strategy, as the objective would be to produce a conveyor belt of such players.

Back with the international team, there now came a chance to succeed at tournament level, when a group of very good players appeared over the next few years. These players, including Steven Gerrard, Paul Scholes, Frank Lampard, David Beckham, Wayne Rooney, Rio Ferdinand and Michael Owen, were christened the golden generation and, along with other good players, formed the basis of some very strong England squads.

What was needed now was the right manager to be appointed, who would develop a team with a system of play and tactics that would realise their potential.

But as Venables and Hoddle were no longer considered acceptable candidates, who was available? Continuing the precedent that England should have an English manager, the FA appointed Kevin Keegan. Keegan had been an outstanding player and serial winner with Liverpool and Hamburg, had 63 caps for England and won two European Golden Boot awards in 1978 and 1979.

As a manager, Keegan started at Newcastle United, who were in some disarray due to internal conflicts and had been relegated to the Second Division. He saved them from relegation to the Third Division (including using his own money to improve the training facilities) and, after the boardroom infighting had been resolved, got them promoted back to the Premier division.

Here, he took them to championship contenders but could not get them over the line. A 12-point lead at the beginning of February was surrendered during the 1995/6 season, when it appeared Keegan was affected by the mind games of Manchester United manager Alex Ferguson, whose side went on to win the title. He never really recovered from this and resigned in 1997. Although he was a popular appointment in 1999 and took England to the 2000 European Championships, he was again found wanting when squandering leads against Portugal and Romania in the group stage and England were eliminated. Keegan resigned in October 2000 after a defeat by Germany in the first game of the 2002 World Cup qualification.

Meanwhile, the golden generation remained mostly intact and still just needed a good manager to organise, motivate and galvanise them into producing performances equal to their talents.

There was talk in the press and among pundits that a foreign manager might bring different methods and tactics more suitable to the international stage. So, after the appointment of two caretaker managers, the FA took that route, not once but twice. What was hoped for was that a foreign manager would marry their understanding of the more technical continental game with the physicality of the English league and produce a hybrid style to succeed at international tournaments.

But without experience of our leagues and a seemingly distant relationship with their players, which appeared to lack inspiration, the experiment was terminated. A suitable system and club-type camaraderie were never really established, and sadly, these ten years with foreign managers (either side of 18 months, with Steve McClaren failing to qualify for the 2008 Euros) were wasted.

A foreign manager with experience and an understanding of the idiosyncrasies of the English game may have been more suitable, but it is not known if this route was explored.

Despite the English press slightly overrating players in some cases as world-beaters, as they have done on several occasions, this was still a collection of outstanding players whose potential was never realised. At a time when we finally had an opportunity to produce a great side, a Venables or Hoddle could have been ideal, but it was not to be.

But this still represented a move in the right direction in terms of the improvement of players' technical abilities at international level. What was needed next time there was a group of players with above-average talent was the right manager to get the best out of them.

This didn't immediately happen, as after a caretaker manager, the two managers who followed were either unable to improve the team's performance or last long enough to even begin.

In May 2012, Roy Hodgson was appointed England manager, with his successful experience of managing both club and national sides all over Europe counting in his favour. Harry Redknapp, who had built a deserved reputation of building teams who passed the ball and played with attacking intent, was also popular with fans and the press but was not considered. During his tenure, Hodgson was unfortunately unable to create a winning style or lift the quality of play of the England team. He resigned after reaching only one quarter-final in the three tournaments he was in charge for. Gareth Southgate, who oversaw the under-21 side, then turned down the England senior team job.

The FA now arrived at a decision to appoint Sam Allardyce. Although he won his first match in charge of the national side, he resigned after this one game for off-field reasons. With all of this, it seemed the FA still lacked a long-term management plan for the international team.

However, when again offered the senior team on Allardyce's resignation in 2016, Southgate initially accepted on a four-match temporary basis and was then subsequently appointed on a full-time contract in November 2016. He went on to qualify England for the 2018 World Cup.

As a player, he started as a fullback and then moved to midfield, playing for Crystal Palace before moving to Aston Villa, converting to centre back and winning international recognition. He was ambitious and so moved again to Middlesbrough, where Steve McClaren was manager and also an England coach. During this period, he became captain and lifted Middlesbrough's first trophy in 128 years when defeating Bolton Wanderers in the 2004 Football League Cup Final.

When McClaren left Middlesbrough to manage England, Southgate was appointed temporary manager of the club, due to his not having the required coaching qualifications. He was given the opportunity by the FA to take his coaching badges while managing and was eventually appointed on a permanent basis in 2006. A decision the FA deserve credit for.

As an international player, he benefited from playing under both Venables and Hoddle and went through the agony of losing a European Championship semi-final on penalties. These penalty-missing moments are character-forming, and Southgate's desire to heal this wound appears to have motivated him throughout his managerial career. He also played under Sven-Göran Eriksson and noticed that his distant demeanour and failure to create a club-type culture in the squad were detrimental to the England team's chances.

His management record at club level was not particularly successful, but his style and understanding of the game caused Arsène Wenger to suggest Southgate as one English manager who could manage the senior team. Having been relegated with Middlesbrough and promising to achieve immediate promotion back to the Premier League, he was strangely sacked in October 2009, with the club in fourth place in the Championship. Another character-forming event and another wound to heal.

He then spent a few years out of management, which were not wasted, as this period included working at the new Centre of Excellence at St George's Park as elite development manager. In 2013, he re-entered management as coach of the England under-21 side, again with limited success.

But on succeeding Allardyce, he found himself with a strong core of quality players and took England to the 2018 World Cup semi-finals. Here there was disappointment again as a return of the technical shortcomings at this level was exposed. After taking the lead, we lost control of the game as Croatia, with superior technique, dominated most of the possession, allowing them to eventually win in extra time.

But Gareth Southgate is a thoughtful individual and student of the game and has appeared to learn and improve whilst in the job. He is also possessed of dignity and resolve, which he has passed on to his players, and this in turn has put the nation behind him and the team. He has been able to take the core of the squad from 2018, many of whom had experienced big games in the Champions League, and add a very promising crop of young technical players, including Jack Grealish and Phil Foden, who were starting to impress in the Premier League. These young players play without fear and, due to their technical excellence, have enormous self-confidence. He also paid particular attention to improving the mental attitude of his squad, in terms of winning for themselves, each other and the nation, on the way creating the best club spirit in any England squad for decades.

GARETH SOUTHGATE

This alignment of the stars produced a very strong, confident squad and resulted in England reaching the final of the 2020 European Championship, played at Wembley. Here, Southgate played a counterattack system that successfully navigated the group stage and a good round of 16 defeat of Germany. But after demolishing a poor Ukrainian side in the quarter-final and somewhat struggling against Denmark in the semi-final, Southgate seemed unwilling to change for the final against Italy, who had overcome the likes of Belgium and Spain to reach the final. And unfortunately, the strength on the bench was either used too late or not at all.

There was a sense of déjà vu in the result, as having taken the lead with a fine goal, England were unable to control the game by keeping the ball. The Italians mostly controlled possession for the rest of the game, gained an equaliser and eventually won via the dreaded English nemesis of penalties.

Watching Spain during this tournament was a delight. They played some of the best football at the tournament, without superstars, just technical players in every position, able to dominate possession against anyone, even Italy, before succumbing on penalties. And although Hungary and Holland had failed to win a World Cup, the final leg of my football trilogy, Spain, had between 2008 and 2012 won a World Cup and two European Championships with their wonderful version of possession football built around the core of the great Barcelona side. A system that continuously produces this type of football is always going to challenge at the highest level.

It must also be said that after failing to qualify for the 2018 World Cup, Italy instigated a bottom-up analysis of what was wrong and, within two years, produced a team and manager to win the 2020 European Championship. When you have an existing conveyor belt of technical talent producing such players, these things are possible!

For England, it's impossible to ignore that the World Cup semi-final and European Championship final were lost in the same fashion, and this goes all the way back to the games against Hungary in 1954. Because we can't keep the ball and control games at the highest level, good fortune is an elusive friend.

This ultimate technical ability of being able to control and pass the ball and so dominate possession at this level is still missing. Southgate and future managers must be much braver with their coaching and trust the players to take the game to opponents and win or lose with their technical ability rather than the cautious approach adopted in this tournament with the sadly predictable outcome. But these two losses at the later stages of top international tournaments represent progress, and England must now take the biggest step and finally win one.

THE FUTURE

The penny is finally dropping. The last 20 years or so have seen welcome progress.

1/ Many younger players, teachers and those working in sports and youth centres are obtaining coaching qualifications

Basic coaching qualifications are now concentrated on the development of the youngest players at the grassroots level in terms of technique and increasing their playing time on small pitches. Above the basic FA 1 and 2 levels, the coaching qualifications are aligned with UEFA so that coaches from all nations travel the same course from junior to professional clubs.

These are now required by schools and clubs at all levels. The youngest boys and girls are being shown the correct way to improve their technique (hope they find time for a ball and a wall!) by qualified coaches, some of whom are in their late teens and early 20s. Their aim now is solely to improve the kids as players without the need to win anything. A ball per child is now the norm, and no one is standing around waiting their turn.

Training or practice sessions are now planned by considering the young players' ages, their growth spurts and their ability, to ensure their natural progression to the next level. This is so welcome, as young players can throughout this process ask questions and seek advice to help them improve from people who are not that much older than them and have the knowledge to do just that.

2/ The explosion of small pitches

Since the arrival of AstroTurf pitches in Britain (I played on one of the first ones, opened by Dennis Law), they have now contributed to the game at youth level more than anywhere else. While they were popular for some professional clubs to install for many years, the improvement in grass pitch development and maintenance has led to their mostly disappearing from the professional game. However, hockey and other sports still make substantial use of them.

But the proliferation of five-a-side complexes around the country has occurred with the installation of AstroTurf and all-weather surfaces.

The use of these in schools and sport centres has added to the popularity and accessibility of the game for players of all ages during the week and at weekends.

These pitches have greatly contributed to technical improvement, due to the substantial increase in the number of touches players have in the small-sided games played on them. This also produces more tight positions where the need to have a good first touch is important. Keeping games small-sided, on small pitches and with smaller balls for the youngest, should be the programme until the teenage years, with just occasional games on a full-size pitch for kids to enjoy.

3/ Fewer competitions

There is now an understanding that junior-level football should be a means to an end, in that players' abilities should be brought along steadily to peak in the late teens to early 20s. More improvement will follow with experience and the determination of the individual to keep learning.

Competitions are necessary in some form to allow the natural desire to compete and win to be released and experienced. This basic instinct exists in some more than others and is important in forming winning mentalities in individuals and teams. And small-sided games are just the thing to nurture these instincts. From memory, five-, six- or seven-a-side games were very competitive. Conditioning sessions to "winning team stay on", as we all know, made things even more interesting!

Speaking earlier of Centres of Excellence, we have had over the years 92 and more of these we didn't realise we had. Another previous argument relating to our poor performance at international level had been that there were too many professional clubs, causing the talent level to be watered down. This in turn allowed too many below-average players to make it into the professional ranks. But what was considered a problem could have been turned into a solution. Because for many years the 92 league clubs' facilities and coaches were underutilised when it came to developing the very youngest players.

Imagine the excitement of any 5- or 6-year-old walking with their mum or dad into any professional club, with the stands, floodlights, etc., and then being taught the game in the right way by qualified coaches in that stimulating environment.

This is now happening much more extensively, where many of these 92 league (and many non-league) clubs are now running programmes for the younger kids from 5 and 6 upwards. This will improve their technical ability at the right age and hopefully produce yet more highly skilled young players for the professional and international ranks.

The big development in football in recent years has been the speed of play. The technical levels of teams and players' abilities are being applied by leading clubs and nations in a more dynamic and high-risk fashion.

Teams now live on the edge with their play, with the ball being passed forward quicker and passes sometimes travelling like shots to teammates, making the first touch more important than ever. The technique of individual players is now tested to the limit when receiving the ball and playing one-twos and other intricate moves. Defensively, presses are now applied at speed and run the risk of being outnumbered if played through. Players are now required to be even fitter and more intelligent, as these systems of play result in both physical and mental fatigue at the end of games. The top clubs are prepared to gamble more on the technical ability of their players to be successful against any type of defence, and it is good to watch and good for the game.

The future is bright if the current course is maintained and technical ability levels continue to improve from the grassroots level upwards. It must also be acknowledged by the English authorities that the game never stands still and is now reaching another level, and we must continuously adapt to meet the challenge.

The change in coaching methods, accessibility to small pitches and the reduction in competitions in the younger age groups are producing results. When looking at the quality in the whole England squad at the 2020 Euros, including the strength of the subs bench and even those who received no playing time, it is very encouraging that England has a group of players to compete at the highest international level for some years to come.

These are the first off the conveyor belt if you like, and it is so important that others are following through the system to sustain the progress now being made.

What must not be forgotten in all this is the economic benefit to be gained from a home-grown system constantly producing high-quality technical players. Spending £50–100m on foreign players to fill a need is not within every club's budget, so getting the coaching right at grassroots level can pay enormous financial dividends later.

What is almost as important now is a conveyor belt of top-quality English managers. The so-called top six of the Premier League – Manchester City, Manchester United, Liverpool, Chelsea, Arsenal and Tottenham – are all currently managed by foreign coaches. English managers appear to be employed to manage clubs for either Premier League security or survival. This must change!

Young managers, much the same as young players, can be influenced by the achievements of others, and it is hoped that as young coaches become young managers, they recognise and understand how successful managers achieve their results, then marry their ideas with those of the best and develop their own identities.

Some managers in Europe have reputations built on good coaching, hard work and organisation with smaller teams, who have been consistent challengers to the established top-tier clubs. Other managers also refer to them when discussing how difficult they are to play against.

Marcelo Bielsa is such an example. His record is not among the most successful managers, but many top players and coaches quote how influential he has been both during their playing and management careers. His multi-dimensional 3-3-3-1 system, which is interchangeable depending on the tactical situation, is a modern take on Total Football, and watching his Leeds side in the Premier division is a very enjoyable experience.

Mauricio Pochettino and Diego Simeone are among those whose own managerial styles have been influenced by Bielsa. Pep Guardiola, one of the greatest modern managers, referred to Bielsa as the best manager in the world in his early days.

From the beginning, the FA have never really sought to appoint an England manager for the sole purpose of winning international tournaments. However, a revolution of some size is now taking place, with recent changes in coaching systems and the Centre of Excellence at St George's Park beginning to bear fruit in terms of young players coming through into the international squad.

These players are of a consistently higher technical standard than seen for many years. It can also be said that Gareth Southgate is a product of all this, as the first manager to come through the system as a manager groomed to win international tournaments. It is now for him and those who follow to be brave and develop a style of play based on controlling the game and possession... They have the tools!

A further sign of the English game recovering its place in world standing will be if, in a decade or so, successful coaches here and abroad refer to one or more English managers who have influenced their style. So here we are looking for the younger coaches now coming through to dare to be different. Not everyone will be successful, but without the shackles of having to base their style on any particular system, some will create a new exciting and winning style, which is taken up by clubs here and abroad.

The hope now is that a combination of top-class players and managers will keep English football at the forefront of the world game, a place that was lost but is being regained. The sole ambition now must be to reach the very top by winning an international tournament, and the World Cup in 2022 would be a wonderful place to start.

As you may have guessed, for me it always has been and always will be about technique. Football is a passing game based on controlling the ball and passing the ball. If you cannot do those, you cannot play it.

So, much to do and much to look forward to...

THANKS AND ACKNOWLEDGEMENTS

FOOTBALLHISTORY.ORG

HISTORY OF FIFA

FA.COM – HISTORY OF THE FA

THE HISTORY OF THE WORLD CUP – CLEMENTE ANGELO

ESSENTIALLYSPORTS.COM

FOOTBALL-STADIUMS.CO.UK

SCHOOLSFOOTBALL.ORG (ESFA)

THEFOOTBALLHISTORYBOYS.COM

FIRSTSPORTZ.COM

FOOTBALLSTADIUMS.CO.UK

ABOHEMIANSPORTINGLIFE.WORDPRESS

DISCOUNTFOOTBALLKITS.COM – BLOG
/FA.COACHING.BADGES.HOW.TO.BE.A.FOOTBALL.COACH

WIKIPEDIA - MULTIPLE

W M FORMATION - By Fallschirmjäger, based on work from Mario Ortegon – Self-made, original file from Mario Ortegon, CC BY 2.5

ERIC CANTONA

INDEX

Nicholson, Bill, 74, 78
Norway, 64
Nottingham Forest, 77, 80
Notts County, 6

Olympic Games, 1908
    inclusion of football in, 7
Olympic Games, 1924, 8
Osgood, Peter, 60
Owen, Michael, 83

Pelé, 35, 37, 39, 56
penalties, 71, 86
Peters, Martin, 38
philosophy, game, 20–8
Platini, Michel, 70
players, in team, 6
Poland, 38
popularity, 5, 6
Portugal, 35, 63, 84
public schools, 4
pundits, 65
Puskas, Ferenc, 23

Ramsey, Alf, 22, 29–40, 74, 77, 78
    retirement, 29
    in Tottenham Hotspur, 29
Real Madrid, 26
Redknapp, Harry, 85
referee, first record of, 5
Regis, Cyril, 81
Rep, Jonny, 44
Revie, Don, 77
Rijkaard, Frank, 62
Roberts, Graham, 81
Robson, Bobby, 81
Robson, Bryan, 60
Romania, 84
Rome
    football-type games in, 3
Rooney, Wayne, 83
Rowe, Arthur, 29, 73–5, 78

rugby, 5
rugby union, 57

Scholes, Paul, 83
schoolboy football, 49–53
Scotland, 5
    game with England, 6
Sebes, Gusztáv, 20, 21, 24
Second World War, 7, 12, 15, 17
Shankly, Bill, 78, 80
Sheffield FC, 5
Shilton, Peter, 77
smaller nations, 63–4
social media, 65
Southgate, Gareth, 85, 86–90
Space – Man – Ball principle, 56
Spain, 20–8, 89
sponsorship, 68
standardisation, 5
Stiles, Nobby, 33

Taylor, Graham, 81
Tigana, Jean, 70
Total Football, 24, 44–6, 56
Tottenham Hotspur, 29, 54, 66–7, 76
Trautmann, Bert, 66
tythe (tax), 3

UEFA, 26
Uruguay, 7, 10, 12
    as World Cup winner, 10

van Basten, Marco, 62
Venables, Terry, 81, 84
Villa, Ricardo, 67

Wales, 38
Warsaw, 1973, 38
Wenger, Arsène, 86
West Germany, 24, 38, 46
Wilkins, Ray, 60
Wilkinson, Howard, 82–3

Lightning Source UK Ltd.
Milton Keynes UK
UKHW020050301121
394794UK00006B/81